REVISITING

The Depths

OVERCOMING

FEAR AND FINDING PEACE

A JOURNEY OF TRANSFORMATION

AMY TAN

AN AWARD-WINNING AUTHOR

Cover photo by Amy Tan, taken at Kampung Tekek, Tioman Island, Pahang, Malaysia.

Cover design by Joshua Crump.

Published in the United States by Books to Hook Publishing, LLC.

Edition: September 2024.

ISBN: 979-8-89283-133-8 (eBook)
ISBN: 979-8-89283-134-5 (Paperback)
ISBN: 979-8-89283-135-2 (Hardcover)
ISBN: 979-8-89283-172-7 (Audiobook)

WINNER OF THE
LITERARY TITAN
GOLD BOOK AWARD
SEPTEMBER 2024

Dedication

To Tioman Island and its underwater world, whose awe inspiring depths and hidden wonders ignited every page of this book. Without their magic, this book would never have been written.

Contents

Chapter 9

Chapter 10

Chapter 11

Chapter 12

AUTHOR'S NOTES

The mesmerizing experience of revisiting the depths of Tioman Island ignited a passion within me to write this book—a chronicles journey of healing, resilience, self-discovery, and transformation that I am passionate about sharing with you. Each chapter reflects these themes, imbued with the enchantment of the underwater world. I hope my story will resonate with you, evoking a sense of connection and inspiring your own unique journey, whether it be through immersing yourself in nature or delving within.

In gratitude for the breathtaking beauty of our underwater world, I am honored to dedicate a portion of the royalties from this book to the marine conservation on Tioman Island.

Diving has revealed to me both the resilience and delicate fragility of our oceans. By supporting this book, you are contributing to vital conservation efforts, helping to preserve these precious ecosystems for us and our future generations to marvel at.

INTRODUCTION

THE RETURN TO THE ISLAND

Returning to the ocean after thirty years was an emotional journey for me, both nostalgic and surreal.

As the island came into view, it felt as if Tioman Island itself was calling me back, beckoning my heart. Situated off the east coast of Peninsular Malaysia in the South China Sea, this island is Malaysia's best-kept secret—a geological wonder, an ecological paradise, and home to pristine rainforests surrounded by warm, sandy beaches, coral reefs, lush seagrass beds, abundant marine life, thriving mangrove forests, and cascading waterfalls.

Its turquoise blue sea glistened invitingly, and you could see marine life, including colorful fish, swimming in its crystal-clear water right from the shoreline. The island's coastline is dotted with powdery golden white beaches, each more inviting than the last, with the sand feeling soft and warm underfoot. Palm trees sway gently in the breeze, their fronds rustling softly, providing natural shade from the tropical sun.

Located 32 nautical miles from the mainland, it is only accessible via ferry from the coastal town of Mersing, Johor and Tanjung Gemuk, Pahang. Once hailed as one of the world's most beautiful beaches by TIME magazine in the 1970s, it has not lost its charm, offering a timeless escape into nature's embrace.

The stroll to the dive site from the marine park was mesmerizing, connected by a long bridge along the ocean. The sea breeze caressed my face and gently flipped my hair, the fresh scent of the ocean mixed with the earthy aroma of the rainforest filled the air, the rhythmic sound of waves crashing against the rocks, and the sunshine reflecting off the ocean's surface was all too familiar and calming to the soul—as if the island and I shared a deep, unspoken connection.

This is it—this was the very ocean where I once dived, sat on the beach taking in the sunset, gazed into the horizon, enveloped in the peace of nature, and cried my heart out to heal my young, fragile, wounded heart. I am back, but now as a resilient, strong woman.

As we approached the dive site to begin my refresher course, a flurry of emotions stirred within me. The salty breeze carried memories of my younger self—excited, fearless, and eager to explore the underwater world. Back then, diving was more than just a hobby; it was a desire to grow and find meaningful connection that filled my heart. The ocean was my sanctuary, where I sought solace.

The waves were ferocious. I wondered how my husband had braved these fierce waves to do his PADI Confined Water exercises. He had arrived on the island a few days before our daughter and me to begin his certification process. A pang of worry gripped my heart, imagining the difficulty he must have faced navigating the oxygen tank, BCD, regulators, fins, and mask for the first time while completing those challenging exercises.

On the morning of his first confined water session, he had told me about the ferocious waves. Standing at the edge of the shore, watching the relentless waves crashing against the rocks, he experienced a surge of anxiety. The ocean's roar was intimidating, a powerful reminder of nature's might. He described the moment he first dipped into the water, feeling the sea's cold embrace. The weight of the equipment was overwhelming, and each piece was an essential component he had to understand and control.

His initial attempts were clumsy; the tank felt heavy, and the regulator seemed unnatural. He struggled with the BCD and the weight belt, which didn't seem to hold securely to his waist, trying to find the right air balance to achieve neutral buoyancy. His heart raced whenever he had to clear his mask or perform a regulator recovery exercise. He confessed how he had momentarily panicked when water seeped into his mask, clouding his vision and making him disoriented.

His experience reminded me of my first dive as if it were yesterday. The moment I descended into the ocean, a wave of excitement and nervousness engulfed me. Adjusting to the weight of the equipment and the sensation of being submerged, I quickly realized that diving was not just a physical endeavor but also a mental journey. The challenges I faced underwater tested my limits and forced me to confront my deepest fears.

The first time I encountered strong currents, it took every ounce of mental fortitude to stay calm and navigate through them. Moments of discomfort, like the pressure on my ears, water entering my mask, the dryness of my mouth from breathing through the regulator, the disorientation caused by low visibility, maintaining neutral buoyancy, and managing the weight of the diving equipment, all became part of the experience.

Yet, with each obstacle I overcame, a powerful sense of triumph surged within me. These experiences taught me that diving demanded not just physical strength but a resilient mindset, the ability to stay calm, and unwavering determination.

This journey beneath the waves mirrored life's challenges, highlighting the empowering feeling that comes with conquering adversity. Life, much like diving, presents us with unforeseen challenges and uncertainties. Before we can enjoy our successes, we must first battle through the difficulties. But with resilience, determination, and the courage to persevere, we can emerge stronger and more resilient. The triumph feels even more rewarding once we break through the barriers, transforming every challenge into a victory.

I reminisced about the carefree days of my youth when the world seemed vast and full of possibilities. I was brimming with dreams and ambitions, eager to carve out my place in the world and form meaningful connections with others. Little did I know then how much the passage of time would shape me.

Life took me on unexpected journeys at a young age—a journey into motherhood, navigating the complexities of entrepreneurship, and embracing the role of a supportive wife while also focusing on my intellectual, emotional, and spiritual development. Juggling these roles was difficult; each added depth and complexity to my life story, leaving unique marks on who I am today.

Motherhood softened me, teaching me patience and unconditional love as I nurtured my children through their various stages of development. I deeply felt their joys and pains, knowing I couldn't shield them from life's challenges. Moments of self-doubt often crept in— Had I given my best? Could I have done better? Did I impact my children positively, or did my fears and prejudices affect them negatively?

Entrepreneurship hardened me, exposing me to the harsh realities of business and the resilience needed to navigate challenges, financial uncertainties, and setbacks. Subsequently, taking up a role in the corporate C-Suite further exposed me to the often harsh realities of corporate life. I had to make decisions and align with the leadership, and these decisions usually hurt me deeply and did not align with my value system. The lack of ethical considerations and long-term vision disheartened me.

However, B Corporations offer a glimmer of hope. My perspective shifted when I learned about them—businesses that balance purpose and profit. B Corps are legally required to consider the impact of their decisions on their workers, customers, suppliers, community, and the environment.

They are committed to using business as a force for good, striving to reduce inequality, lower poverty levels, create a healthier environment, and build stronger communities.

The idea that businesses could contribute positively to society and the planet resonated deeply with me, and I wanted to be part of this movement, or at least adopt its principles. I needed to hold on to something meaningful.

Embracing the role of a supportive wife empowered me, fostering a partnership built on trust, communication, and mutual respect. Balancing individual aspirations with collective goals presented its challenges. I often wondered if I had been the support my partner needed and what kind of pain I might have caused him on our journey together.

Yet amidst the busyness of life's demands, the ocean's call remained a distant echo, a reminder of a part of myself that had been temporarily set aside.

It was surreal to realize that three decades had passed since those early dives. The vibrant memories of my youth contrasted with the responsibilities and challenges of adulthood. Amidst these roles, the longing for the underwater world persisted—a silent yearning that whispered during quiet moments and lingered in dreams. The ocean, once a playground of exploration and freedom, now beckoned with a promise of rediscovery and renewal.

As I prepared for my refresher course and dive once more, I couldn't help but reflect on how these varied experiences had shaped me. They had woven a tapestry of strength, resilience, humility, and empowerment, preparing me to confront the uncertainties that awaited beneath the surface. Now, those same waters held the promise of healing and rediscovery.

As I stood on the boat's deck, gazing at the endless expanse of the ocean, I realized how much I had changed over the years. The young, fearless diver I once was had evolved into a woman shaped by life's experiences—each triumph, setback, joy, and sorrow contributed to the person I had become. The ocean's call was not just a return to a beloved hobby, but a journey back to myself.

The night before the dive, I lay awake in my chalet, listening to the gentle lapping of the waves against the hull. Memories flooded back—my first dive, the sense of wonder as I descended into the blue depths, the thrill of discovering a hidden world beneath the surface. But there were also memories of fear—the panic of losing my mask, the anxiety of navigating strong currents, and the uncertainty of venturing into the unknown.

These memories were a reminder of the duality of the ocean—it could be both a place of beauty and danger, peace and chaos. As I look back on these experiences, I have come to understand that my fear was not something to be ashamed of, but rather a reflection of my courage. Each time I faced my fears, whether underwater or in life, I became more robust and resilient.

The following day, as I donned my wetsuit and checked my equipment, a sense of calm washed over me. The familiar routine of preparing for a dive restored my confidence and gave me a sense of control. My husband, who accompanied us on the boat, offered words of encouragement, reminding me that I was not alone on this journey. His presence provided strength, a constant reminder of the support and love that had always been a part of my life.

As I descended into the water, the initial rush of cold was a shock to my system. However, as I acclimated to the temperature and began exploring the underwater world, a sense of peace enveloped me. The vibrant coral reefs, schools of colorful fish, and the rhythmic dance of the seaweed all contributed to an overwhelming feeling of harmony and balance.

Diving, I realized, was not just about exploring the ocean but about exploring oneself. Each dive was an opportunity to confront fears, push boundaries, and discover new strengths. It was a reminder that growth often came from stepping out of one's comfort zone and embracing the unknown.

As we swam deeper, I reflected on the parallels between diving and life. Both required preparation, awareness, and the ability to adapt to changing circumstances. Both demanded resilience, courage, and a willingness to face challenges head-on. And both offered moments of breathtaking beauty and profound insight.

Emerging from the dive, I experienced a sense of accomplishment and renewal. The ocean had once again proven to be a place of healing and transformation. As we made our way back to the island, I felt a renewed sense of purpose and clarity. The journey was far from over, but I was ready to face whatever lay ahead with confidence and grace.

In the following days, I will continue to dive, expecting each experience to add a new layer to my understanding and appreciation of the ocean and myself. The fears that once held me back were stepping stones to growth and self-discovery. With its vast depths and mysteries, the ocean had become a metaphor for life—a reminder that the most remarkable treasures often lay beyond our comfort zones.

Preparing to leave the island and return to my daily life, I carried the lessons learned from my time in the ocean. The journey of overcoming fear and finding peace was ongoing, a continuous process of reflection and growth. The sea taught me to embrace change, find beauty in the unknown, and trust my resilience.

The experience also deepened my appreciation for the connections that had sustained me through the years. My husband's support, my children's love, and the friendships that had weathered the test of time were all sources of strength and inspiration. These relationships were like anchors, grounding me as I navigated the challenges and uncertainties of life.

I felt an immense gratitude as I stood on the shore, watching the waves crash against the rocks. The ocean had given me a gift—a renewed sense of self, a deeper connection to my inner strength, and a reminder of the beauty and resilience within. The journey of revisiting the depths had not only been a physical one but an emotional and spiritual one as well.

1

MEETING SEBASTIAN AND BEGINNING THE JOURNEY

Upon reaching the dive site, the divemaster, Sebastian, whom my husband had specifically requested, greeted me. Just two months earlier, my husband had decided to take up the PADI Certification and spent an entire day at a dive exhibition, speaking to all the exhibitors. After much consideration, he returned the next day and placed a deposit for a one-on-one guide for me with Sebastian.

I did not know why he chose Sebastian. Perhaps he wanted someone he could resonate with or talk to. He was the catalyst for this trip, making all the transport arrangements, booking my dive and guide, and taking care of every detail. I remember a few nights earlier, before the trip, he was intensely consuming scuba diving material while I fell asleep. Suddenly, I was awoken by his gentle hand caressing my head, and he said, "I will never let you dive without a one-on-one divemaster, my wife." I felt very comfortable; my heart warmed, and I knew I would be in excellent hands. As much as he wanted me to rediscover diving, he likely had his apprehensions, too.

That morning, Sebastian took me through a refresher course in a classroom. As he described scuba diving, he looked up to the right side as if trying to recall a memory, sharing about scuba diving with contagious enthusiasm. His eyes sparked, and his passion radiated throughout our conversation, comforting and inspiring me.

"Diving is all about relaxing and breathing; it's a lazy man's sport," he said, demonstrating with a calm disposition. He described how he would float effortlessly in the water, his breaths slow and deep, creating a sense of calm and relaxation. His movements were fluid and unhurried, embodying the tranquility and ease that diving requires. At that moment, he was momentarily lost in his own world, in a state of being untroubled and tranquil, reflecting inner peace and quiet confidence.

He was an interesting character, reminding me of my younger self when life was carefree and going on one adventure after another.

After the refresher theory, he guided me through selecting my gear. Later, in the pool session, he demonstrated each step with patience and encouragement. Despite my initial nervousness, his confidence and calm demeanor helped me complete the practical session efficiently.

While waiting for our turn to go into the pool for the practical session, I got to know my guide better. In our brief conversation, he shared why he chose to be a divemaster instead of a dive instructor. He wanted to share the love of diving with others, emphasizing that as an instructor, the focus would shift towards certifications and ensuring students gained and passed all required skill sets. This would involve a more structured and regimented approach, with less emphasis on the personal and experiential aspects of diving. In contrast, as a divemaster, Sebastian could focus on guiding divers through their experiences, sharing his passion for the underwater world in a more relaxed and immersive way.

He elaborated that when he was with his family back in the UK, they often asked him when he was coming back to "real life". For Sebastian, diving and interacting with nature embodied his true existence, where he experienced a deep sense of connection to the ocean, and he held the conviction that he could influence individuals' lives by showing them the splendor of the underwater realm.

As I listened to Sebastian, his story made me reflect on the choices people make in life. He had chosen passion over financial gain, valuing experiences over material wealth. His enthusiasm for diving and his love for the underwater world were infectious, making me question the conventional path many of us follow.

Sebastian's life seemed so different from many of us, free from the constraints of corporate life, relentless KPIs, looming deadlines, and the toxic maze of office politics. He had liberated himself from the shackles of debt—no housing mortgages, no car payments, and no credit card debt. Instead, he had found a way to live authentically, moving from one dive site to another, exploring the world's oceans, and sharing that beauty with others. His journey made me wonder about the sacrifices and rewards of such a lifestyle.

Could I ever embrace such a passion-driven life? Would I let go of the security and predictability of a more conventional path? Sebastian's story left me pondering these questions, inspiring me to ruminate on the true meaning of fulfillment and the courage it takes to pursue one's passion.

But then, another question arose: how sustainable is this lifestyle? Will age and the responsibilities of parenthood change this path for Sebastian? Could he maintain his adventurous spirit and freedom once he has a family? Perhaps the natural path would be to start a business surrounding his passion—starting a dive center. Again, this path would present fresh challenges, where passion intertwines with bottom lines and making tough choices. These thoughts lingered as we prepared to head out to enter the pool for the practical refresher session, adding another layer of introspection about the choices we make and the lives we build.

As I immersed myself in the pool, following Sebastian's lead, I practiced the physical skills necessary for the dive and diving deep into my thoughts and emotions. The cool water wrapped around me like a comforting embrace, and with each breath, I felt a bit more of my apprehensions wash away. Sebastian's presence was a steady anchor; his reassuring, encouraging gestures and patient instructions helped me stay focused and calm.

The pool session was more than just a refresher; it was a symbolic step toward confronting my long-held fears. Each task we practiced, from clearing the mask to controlling buoyancy, felt like a small victory. Sebastian's encouraging words echoed in my mind, reinforcing the belief that I could overcome the anxieties that had held me back for so long.

During the breaks, Sebastian shared more about his adventures and the places he had explored. His tales of underwater caves, vibrant coral reefs, and encounters with marine life painted a vivid picture of a magical and intimidating world. His stories were about the beauty he witnessed and the personal growth and insights he gained from each dive.

Listening to Sebastian, I realized that his passion for diving was not just about the act but the deeper connection it fostered with nature and oneself. It was about finding peace and clarity in the depths, away from the noise and chaos of everyday life. His words resonated with me, igniting a spark of curiosity and excitement that had been buried under layers of fear and doubt.

As the session ended, I felt a mix of exhaustion and exhilaration. The physical exertion and the emotional journey left me drained, yet hopeful. Sebastian's parting words,

"You're doing great, keep it up," and "We completed the practical session in just 20 minutes," were a balm to my weary spirit. I knew the real challenge was yet to come, but I was more prepared and determined than ever.

I reflected on the day's events in my chalet that evening. The anticipation of the upcoming dive filled me with nerves and excitement. I jotted down my thoughts in a journal to capture my emotions and insights.

I wrote about Sebastian and his inspiring life, the moments of doubt and fear I had faced, and the small victories that had boosted my confidence. Writing helped me process my feelings, allowing me to see my progress and future journey.

The night was restless, with dreams of underwater worlds and shadowy fears. But amid the turmoil, there were moments of clarity and peace, reminding me of why I had embarked on this journey in the first place. It was not just about conquering fear but about rediscovering a part of myself that I had lost along the way.

Morning arrived with a sense of purpose. As I prepared for the day's dive, I felt a strange calm settle over me. The fear was still there, but a newfound determination accompanied it. I was ready to face the depths, literally and metaphorically, and embrace whatever lay ahead with an open heart and mind.

This trip and meeting Sebastian had been a turning point, a catalyst for change that had set me on a path of self-discovery and healing. His passion and wisdom ignited a spark, challenging me to look beyond my fears and find the courage to pursue my passions. The journey was beginning, but I was fully prepared to immerse myself and discover the depths of my potential.

2

THE NIGHT BEFORE THE FIRST DIVE

That night, sleep eluded me. Lying in bed, a torrent of emotions engulfed me. The ocean had been ferocious today. What if tomorrow is equally bad? Will I panic? What if water gets into my mask and I lose control? What if I choke 50 feet below the seabed? Should I cancel my dive? These lingering doubts finally gave way to an uneasy sleep.

The following day, the sea was calmer, and I was relieved. Yet the previous night had been a relentless mental battle. I lay in bed, staring at the ceiling, my mind racing with questions and what-ifs. The ocean waves crashing against the shore outside my window did little to soothe my anxieties. Instead, they reminded me of the churning, unpredictable nature of the sea.

In the night's stillness, all I could think about were the potential dangers and my fears. Worst of all, I had booked a Discovery Dive for my daughter because I wanted her to experience the underwater world, too. I wanted the three of us to dive together and share this beautiful journey, connecting profoundly through the underwater world. I began to doubt if I had put my precious princess in harm's way.

What if I failed? What if my fears took over, and I couldn't go through with the dive? I closed my eyes and took a deep breath, trying to center myself. Remember why you're doing this, I told myself. This is about rediscovering what was once a sanctuary for you. It's an adventure that you yearned for.

But what if embracing this adventure was too much? What if I wasn't as brave as I used to be? The questions kept coming, an unending spiral of doubt and fear.

In the early morning hours, I must have drifted off into a fitful sleep, my dreams a confusing mix of swirling water and muffled voices. When I awoke, the first light of dawn was filtering through the curtains, and the sound of the waves was gentler, a rhythmic lullaby that signaled a new day.

I got out of bed, feeling a mix of exhaustion and determination. I peeked through the window and saw the sea calmer than it had been the day before. A small wave of relief washed over me. Today might not be as terrifying as I had imagined.

I walked to the balcony, breathing in the salty air. The morning sun painted the sky in shades of pink and orange, a beautiful contrast to the dark thoughts that had plagued me the night before. I watched as a few early risers strolled along the beach; their silhouettes peaceful against the backdrop of the awakening ocean. For a moment, I allowed myself to be absorbed by the tranquility of the scene, letting it soothe my restless mind.

Returning to the room, I found my daughter still asleep, her innocent face serene and unaware of the turmoil within me. I smiled softly, brushing a strand of hair from her forehead. Her presence reminded me why I had embarked on this journey. It wasn't just about facing my fears; it was about creating memories with her, sharing the beauty of the underwater world, and teaching her the importance of overcoming obstacles.

As I prepared for the day, I tried to focus on the positive aspects of the upcoming dive. I reminded myself of the excitement I had felt when I first agreed to this trip, the anticipation of rediscovering a part of myself that had been lost for so long. I thought about the vibrant marine life we would encounter, the sense of weightlessness underwater, and the thrill of adventure. These thoughts brought a calm, albeit fleeting feeling, to my anxious heart.

Breakfast was a quiet affair. My daughter sensed my unease and tried to cheer me up with her infectious enthusiasm. She talked about the fish and turtle she hoped to see, the colors of the coral reefs, and how excited she was to share this experience with me. Her contagious excitement filled me with a brief glimmer of hope.

We met my daughter's dive instructor, Billy, at the dive center and walked to the boat together, where we met Sebastian, the divemaster. His warm smile and confident demeanor were reassuring. He went over the plan for the day, explaining the safety procedures and what to expect during the dive. He shared a charming story about a particular puffer fish that had become his friend and would come to him because it knew he loved it.

When Sebastian described how he would touch the fish, he gestured with his hand as if he were actually caressing it with so much love and care—he had momentarily drifted into his own world of affection with his beloved puffer fish. His enthusiastic love story, along with his calm and patient explanations, helped ease some of my fears, though lingering doubts still lurked in the back of my mind.

Sebastian might have noticed my apprehension. "It's going to be great; you guys have two of the best instructors guiding you," he said gently. "Just remember to breathe. Diving is about trust—trust in yourself, your equipment, and your dive buddy. Remember, you're not alone in this. We'll take it step by step." His words resonated with me. Trust. It was a simple yet powerful concept I had struggled with for so long. Trusting myself, my abilities, and the process was something I needed to embrace if I was to conquer my fears.

As we suited up, I couldn't help but feel a sense of anticipation mixed with dread. The dive gear felt familiar and foreign, a reminder of past experiences and the uncertainties ahead. On the other hand, my daughter was brimming with excitement, her eyes wide with wonder as she inspected her equipment.

We made our way to the dive site, the rhythmic sound of the waves a constant companion. The journey to the dive site was filled with silence and sporadic conversation. My daughter chatted animatedly with Billy, her curiosity and enthusiasm contrasting with my inner turmoil.

When we arrived at the dive site, I took a moment to absorb the surroundings. The water was a brilliant shade of turquoise blue, inviting yet intimidating. The sun sparkled on the surface, creating a mesmerizing dance of light. It was a beautiful day for a dive, but my heart pounded with trepidation.

Sebastian gave us a final briefing, sharing with us the technique to enter the water and the importance of staying calm. As we prepared to enter the water, I took a deep breath to steady my nerves. This was it—the moment of truth.

As we descended into the water, the familiar weightlessness enveloped me. The underwater world came into view, a vibrant tapestry of colors and life. Fish darted around us, their movements graceful and serene. The coral reefs were a riot of hues, teeming with marine creatures. It was a sight to behold, a reminder of the beauty beneath the surface.

But with every breathtaking sight, my fears lingered. The pressure of the water, the unfamiliar sounds, and the realization of how small and vulnerable I was in this vast underwater world weighed heavily on me. I clung to Sebastian's guidance, his presence a reassuring anchor in the depths.

As we continued our dive, I focused on my breathing, the rhythmic inhale and exhale a lifeline to calm my racing heart. I reminded myself of Sebastian's words — trust. Trust in myself, and in the journey. Slowly, I felt a shift within me. The fear dissipated, replaced by a sense of wonder and curiosity.

We reached a point where Sebastian signaled for me to pause. He pointed to a group of fish swimming nearby, their movements synchronized and fluid. It was a mesmerizing sight, a reminder of the harmony in this underwater world. At that moment, I felt a sense of peace and connection to the environment and myself.

As we ascended to the surface, I couldn't help but feel a sense of accomplishment. I had faced my fears, confronted the doubts that had plagued me, and embraced the adventure. It was a small victory, but it was significant. It was a step towards healing, towards finding peace within myself.

Back on the boat, my daughter was bubbling with excitement. She talked about the turtle, fish, and coral and how incredible the dive had been. Her joy was infectious, and I couldn't help but smile. It was all about creating memories, sharing experiences, and finding strength in the journey.

As we headed back to the shore, I felt a sense of gratitude. I was grateful for the experience, Sebastian's support, and the opportunity to share this journey with my daughter. It was a reminder that fear and doubt were a part of the process, but they didn't have to define it.

I reflected on the day's events as I lay in bed that night. A sense of calm and fulfillment replaced the fear and anxiety that had gripped me. With my husband's support, I had taken a step towards healing, rediscovering a part of myself that had been lost. It was a journey of self-discovery, facing fears, and finding peace.

As I drifted off to sleep, I felt a sense of hope. Hope for the future, the adventures ahead, and the journey of healing and self-discovery. The night before had been a battle, but it had also been a turning point. It was a reminder that fear was a part of the journey, but it didn't have to define it.

The journey began, and I was ready to embrace it, one step at a time.

3

THE DAY OF THE DIVE

The anticipation built with each step as we headed to the dive site. The morning sun cast a golden hue over the landscape, bathing everything in a warm, ethereal light. I met with my daughter's instructor, Billy, and urged him not to be adventurous. My daughter's safety came first, and I emphasized we had plenty of time and could always come back if we couldn't achieve our objectives. He gave me a reassuring smile, nodding to signal that he understood and assured me that the dive was not deep.

As we boarded the boat, I felt a strange mix of fear and exhilaration. The calm sea was a good omen, a silent promise of a smoother journey ahead.

As we moved away from the shore, the boat gently rocked, and the rhythmic sound of the waves soothed my nerves. The air was filled with the salty tang of the ocean, a scent that brought back memories of my earlier diving days. I watched my daughter's excitement grow, her eyes sparkling with the same adventurous spirit that had once burned within me.

Our gear was all well-prepared and arranged. The wetsuits, fins, and masks were laid out meticulously, demonstrating the careful planning and attention to detail that diving demanded. Sebastian gathered us for a final briefing, his calm demeanor and confident voice providing stability and reassurance. Sharing vital information, the other divemaster onboard emphasized safety protocols and what to expect underwater.

The anticipation built up as I put on my dive gear, each piece a familiar friend yet a poignant reminder of the time that had passed. The weight of the tank on my back was both physical and symbolic—a tangible link to my past self and a gateway to reconnect with the depths that had once been my sanctuary. I watched my daughter as she suited up; her enthusiasm was infectious. Her laughter and chatter lightened the mood, making the impending dive less daunting.

However, along with excitement, there was also an undercurrent of apprehension. Over the years, fear had stealthily crept in where once there was only daring bravery. Once exhilarating, the vastness of the ocean now harbored a hint of trepidation. Would I still possess the courage to dive into its depths and confront the uncertainties beneath the ocean? I took a deep breath, trying to calm the storm of thoughts swirling in my mind.

As we neared the dive site, Sebastian pointed out landmarks to guide us underwater. The boat slowed to a stop, and we prepared for entry. The water looked inviting, its surface shimmering under the sunlight.

Sebastian took the first plunge, waiting for me at the surface, while Billy remained on the boat to assist us. I was next, followed by my husband

and daughter. The cool water enveloped me in its familiar yet foreign embrace.

As I adjusted to the underwater environment, the initial shock of the water transformed into a sense of calm. The sounds of the world above faded, replaced by the gentle hum of the ocean. I focused on my breathing, each inhale and exhale a reminder to stay present, to let go of my fears and embrace the moment. Sebastian's presence beside me was a constant source of comfort, his experienced eyes scanning the surroundings, ensuring everything was as it should be.

We descended slowly, the colors of the underwater world coming to life with each meter we went deeper. The coral reefs were a vibrant tapestry of life, teeming with fish of all shapes and sizes. I watched in awe as schools of fish moved in perfect harmony, their movements synchronized, as if performing a delicate ballet. The sight was mesmerizing, a reminder of the beauty hidden beneath the surface.

As we continued our descent, I felt a sense of connection with the ocean that I had long forgotten. The fears that had once plagued me began to dissipate, replaced by a sense of wonder and curiosity. The deeper we ventured, the greater sense of peace enveloped me. It was as if the ocean was welcoming me back, its depths offering a sanctuary from the chaos of the world above.

Sebastian led me to a stunning section of the reef, where the coral formations were intricate and delicate. The play of light and shadow created a surreal atmosphere, as if we had stepped into another realm. We paused to take in the surrounding beauty, the silence of the ocean amplifying the moment. It was in this stillness that I found a sense of clarity, a realization that the fears I had carried for so long were no longer a burden.

We continued to explore, each turn revealing new wonders. The underwater world was a treasure trove of surprises, from the smallest nudibranch to the majestic baby shark gliding effortlessly through the water. Each encounter was a reminder of the resilience and adaptability of life, showcasing the beauty of the natural world.

As our dive time came to an end, we began our ascent; the surface growing closer with each kick. The journey back was filled with a sense of accomplishment and relief. Breaking through the surface, I was greeted by the warmth of the sun and the sound of laughter. My daughter's joy was contagious, and her excitement reflected the shared experience that had brought us closer together.

Back on the boat, we debriefed, sharing our impressions and highlights of the dive. The sense of camaraderie was palpable, a bond forged through the shared adventure. As we made our way back to shore, an intense sense of gratitude overwhelmed me. The dive had been more than just a physical journey; it had been a journey of the soul, a rediscovery of courage and resilience.

The day of the dive had been a turning point, a moment of transformation. It was a reminder that the fears we carry are often of our own making and that facing them can lead to remarkable healing and growth. As I watched the shoreline come into view, I knew that this was just the beginning. There would be more dives, more challenges, and more opportunities to confront and overcome the fears that had once held me back.

In the end, it was not just about diving into the depths of the ocean but about diving into the depths of oneself. It was about finding peace in the face of fear and discovering the strength that lies within. The journey had been long and arduous, but it had been worth every moment. For in the depths, I had found not only the courage to face my fears but also the peace that comes from embracing the unknown.

4

THE DESCENT AND RISING ANXIETY

The back roll entry into the water was thrilling and dramatic, evoking a mix of excitement and apprehension. As I splashed into the water, I was momentarily enveloped in a cool embrace, the sensation both comforting and daunting.

Sebastian asked, "How do you feel?" to which I replied, "I am excited and nervous at the same time."

The chill of the water sent a shiver down my spine, awakening every nerve in my body, making me acutely aware of the fine line between exhilaration and fear. The ocean's vast expanse stretched out before me, its surface a glistening mirror reflecting the sunlight, while beneath lay the unknown depths I was about to explore.

As we began our descent, the world around me transformed. The vibrant blues and greens of the ocean above gave way to deeper, darker hues. The light filtering down created a mesmerizing dance of shadows and highlights, a visual symphony that both enchanted and unnerved me. Each movement of my fins seemed to disturb the delicate balance of this underwater ballet, sending ripples through the water that echoed my inner turmoil.

Despite my efforts to remain calm, a rush of traumatic memories flooded back. The sensation of water entering my nose after clearing my mask heightened my anxiety. We had barely descended twenty percent of the way down, yet my unease was overwhelming. How is this possible? I have done this before without panic. What is happening to me? These questions echoed in my mind, their relentless rhythm mirroring the increasing pace of my heartbeat. I felt a tightening in my chest, a familiar sign of the panic that had often gripped me in the past.

At my request, we surfaced briefly to allow me to regain my composure. The transition from the eerie silence of the deep to the vibrant noise of the surface was jarring. I felt the weight of my past pressing down on me, a tangible force that seemed to pull me back into the depths of my memories. The memory of my first PADI licensing with Rick thirty years ago resurfaced vividly. His disapproving, mean, and angry face haunted me, and I could almost hear him screaming at me underwater. His words, sharp and cutting, echoed through my mind, each one a reminder of my perceived failures and shortcomings.

It startled me to realize how deeply those moments had imprinted on me. The fear and shame that had consumed me were still very much a part of me, lurking just beneath the surface, ready to rise at the slightest provocation. I couldn't help but wonder if this resurgence of emotions was a form of PTSD triggered by my return to diving or just my fear of the unknown. The line between the two was blurred, each feeding into the other in a vicious cycle that seemed impossible to break.

As I floated on the surface, my eyes closed against the glare of the sun, I took several deep breaths, trying to calm the storm of emotions within me. Sebastian asked, "Why are you panicking?"

I responded, "There's a lot of water, and I can't seem to clear my mask."

"You are in the ocean; there will be a lot of water. Get used to it. Just trust me," he said. "Let's try again."

The rhythmic sound of my breathing, amplified by the regulator, became a focal point, a steadying force amidst the chaos. I reminded myself of the reasons I had returned to the water, the desire to conquer my fears and find peace, to reconnect with a part of myself that I had long ignored.

Sebastian, ever patient and understanding, floated beside me, offering silent support and giving me the time I needed to compose myself. His urging to trust him and his reassuring presence was a comforting reminder I was not alone on this journey. With renewed determination, I signaled I was ready to try again.

As we descended once more, and this time we succeeded, I watched as the world above slowly dimmed. The vibrant colors of the surface faded into the subdued hues of the deep. Each sight was a reminder of the wonder and mystery of the ocean, a counterbalance to the fears that threatened to overwhelm me.

The deeper we went, the more surreal the world became. The play of light and shadow created an almost dreamlike atmosphere, a place where reality seemed to blur and merge with my memories and emotions. I felt as though I was moving through a living painting, each brushstroke a representation of my journey, both past and present. The buoyancy of my scuba gear made me feel weightless—a stark contrast to carrying the same equipment on land, which was a constant reminder of the physical challenge. Yet, it also served as a symbol of the burdens I carried within me.

At one point, we came across a stunning section of the reef, teeming with life and color. Sebastian pointed out various species of fish, his excitement evident even through the muffled sounds of the underwater world. I tried to focus on his enthusiasm, to let it pull me out of my introspection and into the present moment. It worked, if only for a while, as I allowed myself to be drawn into the beauty of the scene before me.

Yet, despite the distractions, my mind kept returning to Rick and the events of thirty years ago. His harsh words and critical demeanor had left deep scars, shaping my perceptions and fears in ways I was only now beginning to understand. It dawned on me that this dive was not just about overcoming a fear of the unknown, but about confronting the deeper issues that I had kept buried for so long. It was about reclaiming my sense of self, of proving to myself that I was capable and strong.

As we continued our descent, I experienced a gradual shift within me. The initial panic began to subside, replaced by a growing sense of determination. I focused on my breathing, on the steady rhythm that had always been a source of comfort. I reminded myself of the training I had undergone and the skills I had mastered. I was not the same person I had been thirty years ago. I had grown, learned, and evolved. This dive was an opportunity to acknowledge that growth, to see myself not through the lens of past failures, but through the achievements and strengths I had gained over the years.

By the time we reached our intended depth, a sense of calm had replaced the panic. The world around me, once a source of fear, had become a place of serenity and beauty. The colors seemed brighter, the movements more fluid. I experienced a connection to the ocean that had been absent for years, a feeling of belonging that was both unexpected and incredibly comforting.

We spent several minutes exploring the reef, each moment a step further away from the shadows of my past. Sebastian signaled for us to begin our ascent, and I felt a mix of relief and pride. I had faced my fears and come out on the other side, stronger and more resilient. As we broke the surface, the sunlight warm on my face, I knew this dive had been a turning point. It had shown me that the past, while a part of me, did not define me. I had the power to shape my future, to move forward with confidence and courage.

Back on the boat, I took a moment to reflect on the experience. The journey was far from over, but I had taken an important step. I had faced my fears and found a measure of peace. The ocean, with all its beauty and mystery, had become a place of healing. I looked forward to the dives to come, not just as a challenge to be overcome, but as opportunities for growth and self-discovery. The depths I had once feared had become a source of inspiration, a testament to the power of resilience and the human spirit.

5

THE DEPTHS OF TRUST

With Sebastian's insistence on trusting him and his calm demeanor reassuring me, we made a second attempt. This time, we descended successfully. As we ventured deeper, I couldn't escape the resurgence of inadequacy and terrifying moments from my first PADI licensing experience.

I vividly recounted the incident when I was completing the PADI Open Water Certification. It was an exercise where we were required to remove all our equipment (BCD, regulator, and mask) under the fifty-foot seabed while kneeling down, then assemble everything back together and use the compass to navigate ourselves to a point near the boat before ascending.

Four of us descended together to start this exercise, but I was the last. I watched as, one by one, my dive mates completed the exercise effortlessly. My heart pounded each time one of them finished and swam away.

I couldn't help but wonder why Rick didn't let me go first since I was the only lady and the weakest among the group. However, by the time it was my turn, I had composed myself and was determined to excel.

The exercise site was stark, with hardly any reef or sea creatures—just the vast emptiness of the sea stretching out into silence. During the exercise, my instructor maintained a distance, observing from at least ten feet away. I took a deep breath and methodically began my task. First, I calmly removed my BCD, followed by my weight belt, and last, my mask. Methodically, I reassembled everything, starting with the regulator, ensuring it was properly in place, then the weight belt. Next, I donned the BCD, and finally, I repositioned and cleared my mask.

Bravo, I made it. A sense of triumph washed over me.

However, as I completed my exercise and prepared to use the compass to navigate, a sudden unease gripped me—I couldn't see my instructor anywhere.

Frantically gazing left, right, front, and back, I couldn't find him. That moment sent shivers down my spine. In the sea's vastness, I felt utterly alone and petrified.

Why would Rick leave me alone? Where is he? Why didn't he assure me that in this exercise, I would be alone, but he would be nearby watching? Why didn't he let me go first?

I assured myself by thinking that he was somewhere watching, perhaps testing me to handle situations where I would be completely alone and able to save myself.

Composing myself and reminding myself to stay calm, I knew I needed to complete the exercise. I had to succeed; failure was not an option. Braving my deep fear and insecurity, I began to use the compass. Despite my uncertainty about the direction, I pushed forward, determined to succeed despite the overwhelming trepidation.

Finally, uncertain about the compass's direction, I ascended. When I surfaced, I was too far from the boat, and the ocean current was ferocious. I tried desperately to swim back towards the boat, but the relentless ocean pushed me further away.

With the current at my back and kicking with all the energy I could muster, I fought my way towards the boat.

As I struggled closer, I heard the thunderous cheers from my friends on the boat. Lydia's voice was the loudest, shouted, "Come on, come on, you will make it! Focus on us. You're almost there. Just a little to go!" Her unwavering encouragement helped me stay focused and brave the ferocious storm. With each stroke I managed, the cheers grew louder, repeating the same phrases, pushing me onward. As I finally approached the boat, everyone erupted in cheers, and the boatman swiftly helped me aboard.

The vulnerability I felt was immense, navigating a flood of emotions while remaining acutely aware of my surroundings and not having the confidence that I could handle a situation should it arise.

I realized I had to break my vulnerability barrier and learn to trust my guide completely, understanding that I was not alone in this dive.

Sebastian's reassuring squeeze of my Pericardium 6, about two to three finger-widths above my wrist, between my two tendons, helped ground me, breaking the grip of those haunting memories.

Although I had never articulated my fear or shared my PADI certification experience beyond my strict diving instructor, who was a military dive trainer, Sebastian was remarkably perceptive and sensitive. It was as if he intuitively understood my fear and knew exactly how to reassure me.

Redirecting my focus, I immersed myself in the mesmerizing allure of the underwater world. For this newfound courage and serenity, I owe a debt of gratitude to Sebastian. His passion, appreciation, and affinity for the underwater world, coupled with his empathy and patience, helped me overcome my fear and gain the confidence I needed.

Could his love for this world below the surface offer insights into human empathy and emotional awareness? As we successfully descended to the seabed, Sebastian checked I was OK and afterward raised his hand with a celebratory victory.

Perhaps it is also challenging for a divemaster to help people filled with emotion and anxiety to dive, as human reactions and actions can be unpredictable under stress. Seeing his gesture, I felt a wave of triumph and solidarity.

This moment was more than just a dive for me; it was a personal journey of overcoming fears and finding strength in trust. Perhaps, for Sebastian, it was yet another achievement to help and show a complete stranger the beauty of the underwater world.

6

IMMERSING IN THE UNDERWATER WORLD - OBSERVATIONS AND REFLECTIONS

At a depth of nine meters, the tranquil ocean enveloped me in a world of quiet splendor. The crystal-clear waters shimmered with an iridescent turquoise blue, illuminated by rays of sunlight piercing through the surface above. As we descended further, the familiar sight of vibrant coral reefs greeted me, but something felt different this time.

The once-lush coral formations seemed less vibrant, their colors muted compared to my memories from decades past. A subtle sadness tugged at my heart as I observed the changes in this underwater landscape.

Climate change and human impacts had taken their toll, leaving behind a stark reminder of the delicate balance between nature's resilience and vulnerability.

The corals that once boasted vibrant shades had turned ghostly white, a sign of coral bleaching. The stark white skeletons of the corals were a haunting testament to the rising ocean temperatures and pollution that have plagued these reefs. Coral bleaching occurs when corals, stressed by changes such as warmer water temperatures, expel the symbiotic algae living in their tissues. This alga, known as zooxanthellae, provides the corals with their color and, more importantly, their primary source of energy through photosynthesis. Without it, the corals turn white and become more susceptible to disease and death.

The muted colors of the remaining coral contrasted with memories of my youth. I remembered the vivid hues of the underwater world—corals in brilliant shades of red, orange, purple, and yellow, teeming with schools of colorful fish. Now, the scene was different. It was as if the vibrancy of the ocean had faded, leaving behind a more somber and reflective landscape.

Despite the subdued colors, life persisted amidst the reef. I marveled at a school of fish encircling a coral reef. They moved in synchronized, circular patterns—a dance that defied the seemingly chaotic world around them. Among the coral, a pair of clownfish darted in and out of their cozy anemone home, their vibrant orange and white stripes a stark contrast against the earthy hues of the reef.

As I drifted along the reef, a deep sense of awe and connection washed over me. The initial apprehension I had felt on the descent had given way to a serene appreciation of the intricate beauty that surrounded me. The ocean, a source of uncertainty earlier, now embraced me with its tranquility and resilience.

The rhythmic sound of my breaths through the regulator blended harmoniously with the gentle currents, creating a symphony of peace and wonder. In these depths, I found myself letting go of any lingering doubts or fears, fully immersed in the present moment and the wonders it held.

In those tranquil depths, I rediscovered a sense of wonder and curiosity that had been dormant for too long. The underwater world offered not only a sanctuary of beauty but also a profound lesson in resilience and interconnectedness.

Near the ocean floor, I came across an unexpected sight—a steel stand, its origins and purpose shrouded in mystery. Its presence raised poignant questions about human impact on the underwater environment. Was it discarded callously, disrupting the natural beauty that thrives here? Or perhaps it was a remnant of a shipwreck, a haunting reminder of past maritime journeys now intertwined with the marine ecosystem.

Despite this intrusion, the steel stand served as an unlikely host for life. Vibrant coral colonies adorned its surface, resiliently clinging to its metal frame. Their colors danced with the currents, a testament to nature's ability to adapt and thrive even in the presence of human artifacts.

At the top right corner of the steel stand, a surprise awaited—a dark orange scarf, carefully tied in a makeshift pocket. Its presence intrigued me. Who had placed it there, and with what intent? Was it a diver's personal touch, a symbolic gesture left behind to honor the ocean's beauty? The scarf, meticulously tied, suggested a thoughtful intention, yet I couldn't help but wonder about its ecological impact. Did the person consider how their gesture might affect the delicate balance of marine life?

As I pondered these questions, my attention was drawn to a pair of medium-sized fish, probably blue-lined snappers, their bodies adorned with bright yellow, sky blue, and grey stripes. They darted playfully through the water, their movements fluid and synchronized. Curiously, they swam towards the scarf, weaving in and out of its fabric as if performing a delicate underwater ballet. The gentle sway of the scarf with each movement created a mesmerizing ripple effect, a harmony of natural grace amidst the steel and coral.

In witnessing this scene, I couldn't help but reflect on our responsibility as stewards of the ocean. The juxtaposition of human artifacts and thriving marine life underscored the delicate balance we must strive to maintain. Each interaction, intentional or unintentional, leaves a mark on this underwater world—a world resilient yet vulnerable.

The steel stand stood as a silent sentinel on the ocean floor, its weathered surface telling the story of years spent submerged in the salty embrace of the sea. As I approached closer, the details of its construction became clearer. Barnacles clung tenaciously to its edges, tiny crustaceans adding their own touch to the structure's rugged appearance. I imagined running my fingers along its cold, smooth surface, imagining the stories it could tell if only metal could speak.

Beyond the steel stand, the reef extended in a tapestry of life. Schools of fish, like shimmering rainbows, darted in and out of coral crevices. Anemones swayed gently with the ebb and flow of the current, their tentacles reaching out in search of passing nutrients. It was a bustling ecosystem, where every creature played a role in the intricate dance of survival.

As my gaze returned to the scarf, its presence continued to intrigue me. I wondered about the diver who had placed it there. Was it an act of reverence for the underwater world, a silent tribute to the beauty that surrounded us? Or perhaps it held a more personal meaning, a memento left behind to mark a significant moment in someone's diving journey.

I reached out to touch the scarf, feeling the softness of its fabric contrast with the hard metal of the stand. It had weathered the ocean's currents with surprising resilience, its color slightly faded but still vibrant against the backdrop of coral and fish. The fish, seemingly unbothered by my presence, continued their graceful ballet around the scarf, as if accepting it as part of their underwater landscape.

In this moment of quiet observation, I found myself contemplating the broader implications of human interaction with marine environments. The scarf, while adding a touch of human presence to the scene, also raised ethical questions about our impact on underwater ecosystems. How does our presence, even in small gestures, influence the delicate balance of marine life? These thoughts weighed heavily as I continued to explore the underwater world, each encounter with marine life deepening my appreciation for its complexity and fragility.

The coral, resilient despite the challenges posed by climate change and human activity, offered a poignant reminder of nature's endurance. Yet, signs of stress were evident—a bleached section here, a damaged colony there. It was a stark contrast to the vibrant corals of decades past, a visual representation of the threats facing our oceans today.

As I floated among the coral formations, I noticed a subtle movement—a sea turtle gliding gracefully overhead, its ancient shell a mosaic of patterns against the azure waters. The turtle seemed unperturbed by my presence, a silent ambassador of the ocean's resilience and beauty. I watched as it disappeared into the distance, a fleeting reminder of the interconnectedness of life below the surface.

Returning to the steel stand, I observed a tiny crustacean scuttling across its surface, oblivious to the larger questions occupying my mind. For this tiny creature, the steel stand was simply home—a safe haven amidst the vastness of the ocean. It reminded me of the resilience of marine life, adapting to challenges imposed by human artifacts with a tenacity that echoed through generations.

In the distance, a faint shadow caught my eye—a school of barracuda, their sleek bodies glinting in the sunlight as they patrolled the reef. They were predators of the deep, their presence a reminder of the delicate balance between predator and prey in this underwater realm. I marveled at their streamlined forms, perfectly adapted to the rigors of ocean life.

Reflecting on these encounters, I realized the importance of responsible stewardship of our oceans. Every dive, every interaction with marine life, carried with it a responsibility to minimize impact and maximize conservation efforts. The steel stand, with its dual role as an artificial reef and a reminder of human presence, symbolized our potential to coexist harmoniously with nature.

As I ascended towards the surface, buoyed by the weightlessness of the water, I carried with me a renewed sense of purpose. The scarf, now a symbol of introspection and ethical consideration, fluttered gently in the current, its presence a reminder of the interconnectedness of all life forms in the ocean. I vowed to continue exploring and advocating for the protection of our oceans, ensuring that future generations could experience the wonder and beauty I had encountered beneath the waves.

7

UNDERWATER BALLET AND BABY SHARK

Suddenly, Sebastian squeezed my hand with palpable excitement and pointed to the right. Following his gesture, I spotted it—a baby shark gliding gracefully along the seabed. Its sleek form moved with an elegance that belied its predatory nature. As it moved, its swift form disrupted the sand momentarily, creating a small flurry of almost powdery sand particles. These particles created a transient cloud-like appearance, reminiscent of a large puff of smoke underwater, though much more subtle and ephemeral.

The sight was captivating. The shark's graceful movement left a trail of gentle disturbance before disappearing into the depths once more.

In that awe-inspiring moment, surrounded by the wonders of the underwater world, I felt a deep connection to the delicate balance of life beneath the waves. Each encounter—from the lively school of fish to the playful clownfish, the graceful balletic pair of fish, the barnacles and tiny crustaceans, the sea turtle, the majestic baby shark, and sporadic vibrant corals amidst the earthy hues—underscored the remarkable diversity and resilience of oceanic life.

As I watched the baby shark vanish into the blue, my thoughts drifted to the significance of this encounter. It wasn't just a sighting of marine life; it was a reminder of nature's elegance and unpredictability. The underwater world, with its intricate ecosystems and symbiotic relationships, mirrored the complexities of human emotions and interactions.

Reflecting on Sebastian's earlier words about the interconnectedness of life underwater, I realized how each creature, from the smallest fish to the apex predators like the shark, played a vital role in maintaining the health of the reef. Their movements, feeding habits, and interactions painted a dynamic tapestry of survival and adaptation.

The underwater landscape shifted with every movement. Sunlight filtered through the water, casting ethereal beams that danced on the sandy bottom. Schools of fish darted around, their scales catching the light and shimmering like scattered jewels. Each species seemed to have its own rhythm, contributing to the underwater symphony of life.

Amid this aquatic ballet, I found myself drawn to a pair of fish engaged in a graceful dance near a cluster of vibrant corals. Their movements were synchronized, almost choreographed, as they weaved in and out of the coral branches. Their colors—a mesmerizing blend of blues and yellows—stood out against the backdrop of muted hues, a true testament to nature's artistry.

The coral reef itself, once teeming with vibrant life, now bore signs of change. Some corals, though still beautiful, showed faint traces of bleaching—a stark reminder of the environmental challenges facing our oceans. Environmentalists had often mentioned and expressed the impact of climate change and human activities on these fragile ecosystems. Seeing it firsthand brought a mix of admiration for nature's resilience and concern for its future.

As we continued our underwater journey, Sebastian pointed out a school of clownfish darting in and out of anemone homes. Their vibrant orange and white stripes contrasted vividly with the subdued tones of the reef. Watching their playful antics, I couldn't help but marvel at their ability to thrive amidst changing conditions.

Each moment underwater deepened my appreciation for the fragility and strength of life beneath the waves. It was more than a dive; it was a voyage of discovery—a reminder of the interconnectedness of all living things and our responsibility to protect these delicate ecosystems.

The encounter with the baby shark, in particular, left an indelible mark on my soul. Its fleeting presence symbolized resilience and adaptability, qualities I hoped to embody as I navigated my journey of healing and self-discovery. In its graceful movements, I saw a reflection of my path—full of challenges yet brimming with possibilities.

The underwater ballet had not only enriched my understanding of marine life, but had also reignited a passion for conservation and advocacy. I vowed to share this transformative experience, hoping to inspire others to appreciate and protect our oceans for generations to come.

8

CONNECTION AND PEACE

Completely immersed in the aquatic realm, an overwhelming sense of peace enveloped me as I embraced its splendor. The only sound was my breathing, rhythmic and soothing in the surrounding vastness. In that perfect silence, I felt an overwhelming sense of love, peace, and acceptance—truly, I felt I had encountered God. This transcendent moment, where time seemed to stand still, was beyond precious.

It made me reflect on why some seek solace, healing, love, and acceptance in the underwater world. This realm serves as a testament to its unparalleled wonder and tranquility. It gently reminded me of our humble place within the grandeur of God's creation.

A powerful sense of belonging and interconnectedness replaced the vulnerability I felt earlier. I realized that this underwater world was not just a physical space, but a spiritual sanctuary where one could find peace and clarity— a familiar feeling that I had longed to rediscover.

As I floated effortlessly, surrounded by the mesmerizing dance of light and water, I felt a deep connection to everything around me. The vibrant colors of the fish, the gentle sway of the seaweed, and the rhythmic patterns of the coral all seemed to pulse with life and energy. It was as if the ocean itself was breathing, and I was part of its breath.

This moment of unity with the underwater world brought a sense of clarity and purpose. I understood why people are drawn to the ocean, seeking its embrace as a refuge from the chaos and noise of everyday life. The underwater world offers a purity and simplicity that is rare and precious. It is a place where one can shed the burdens of the world above and reconnect with the essence of being.

The spiritual awakening I experienced underwater resonated deeply with me. It was a reminder that peace and connection are always within reach, even in the most unexpected places. This journey was not just about confronting my fears and rediscovering a part of myself; it was also about finding a deeper, more meaningful connection to the world around me and to the divine presence that permeates all creation.

The initial rush of fear and exhilaration upon entering the water gradually gave way to a serene stillness. I found myself suspended in a world where time seemed to stretch infinitely, each moment pregnant with meaning. The gentle sway of the seaweed and the vibrant colors of the fish took on new significance, as if each movement and hue whispered secrets of the universe.

In this underwater sanctuary, I was not merely an observer, but an integral part of a living tapestry. The rhythm of my breathing synchronized with the ocean's gentle pulse, creating a harmonious symphony that resonated deep within my soul. It was in this place, surrounded by the interplay of light and shadow, that a strong sense of belonging enveloped me.

As I gazed into the depths, the water shimmered with a thousand reflections, each one a mirror to my innermost thoughts and emotions. I realized that the fears I had carried for so long were not burdens to be cast aside but threads in the intricate fabric of my journey. Each fear conquered was a step closer to understanding, to embracing the fullness of life without reservation.

The silence of the underwater world became a canvas upon which I painted my hopes and dreams, each stroke symbolises my resilience and growth. Here, amidst the vastness of the ocean, I found solace knowing that I was never truly alone. The presence of life in its myriad forms reminded me of the interconnectedness of all beings, a universal truth that transcends time and space.

In the embrace of the ocean's depths, I discovered a clarity that had eluded me for so long. The simplicity of existence beneath the waves offered a stark contrast to the complexities of everyday life above. Here, there were no deadlines to meet or expectations to fulfill—only the gentle ebb and flow of life in its purest form.

As I continued to explore this underwater realm, each moment unfolded like a chapter in a story written by the ocean itself. I marveled at the resilience of the coral reefs, which despite facing unprecedented challenges, continued to thrive and flourish. Their steadfastness mirrored my journey of healing and renewal, demonstrating the power of perseverance in the face of adversity.

In the distance, a school of fish moved as one, their movements choreographed with effortless grace. I watched in awe as they navigated the currents with precision, a living embodiment of unity and harmony. It was here, amidst this symphony of life, that I found answers to questions I had not yet dared to ask.

The underwater world offered more than just a temporary escape—it provided a sanctuary where the boundaries between the physical and spiritual realms blurred. Here, in the depths of the ocean, I felt a connection to something greater than myself—a force that transcended language and comprehension. It was a communion with the divine, a reminder that peace and acceptance are not destinations but ongoing journeys of the heart and soul.

As I reluctantly began my ascent toward the surface, the lessons learned in the depths remained etched in my consciousness. I carried a newfound sense of purpose and a deeper appreciation for the interconnectedness of all life. The underwater world had become more than a place of refuge—it was a beacon of hope and renewal in a world too often overshadowed by doubt and uncertainty.

In that moment of transition, as the sun's rays pierced the surface and illuminated the surrounding water, I made a silent vow to always carry the tranquility of the ocean within me. For in its depths, I had found not only peace but a meaningful connection to the essence of existence itself—a connection that would guide me on my journey long after I had returned to dry land.

9

THE ASCENT AND REFLECTION

As Sebastian signaled for us to ascend, I reluctantly acknowledged it was time to depart from the wondrous underwater realm. The journey upward felt like both a physical and emotional ascent. The shifting light and the sensation of drawing closer to the surface stirred mixed feelings within me—a blend of awe at the underwater world's beauty and a reluctance to leave its serene embrace.

Breaking through the surface, the familiar sights and sounds of the world greeted me above. Sebastian looked pleased with the dive, his eyes sparkling with enthusiasm as he turned to me. "How do you feel?" he asked.

"I feel incredible," I replied, a sense of achievement spreading across my face.

Yet, internally, emotions swirled, making it difficult to articulate them. The dive had been more than a journey underwater; it had been a journey within myself, confronting fears and rediscovering a dormant part of my soul.

With the boat lady's help, I climbed back onto the boat. The sun's warmth enveloped me, contrasting with the cool embrace of the ocean. The gentle sway of the vessel, the laughter of fellow divers, and the joyful chatter of my daughter created a comforting yet disorienting contrast. My husband observed with a beaming smile, sharing in our happiness vicariously. The stark juxtaposition between the tranquility of the underwater world and the bustling activity aboard the boat left me yearning for the peace I had found beneath the waves.

Reflecting on the dive, I felt a deep sense of awe and gratitude for the underwater world's beauty. The vibrant corals, the graceful dance of sea creatures, and the rhythmic ebb and flow of the ocean had touched me deeply. However, alongside this beauty, there was also a sobering sadness. I couldn't shake the image of bleached corals and the delicate balance of the ecosystem, reminders of the human impact on this fragile environment. This mix of awe and sorrow underscored the urgency of protecting and cherishing our oceans, ensuring future generations could experience their wonder.

Upon our return to shore, the gentle rocking of the boat provided a soothing rhythm, allowing me to begin processing my thoughts and emotions. The dive had transcended mere adventure; it had been a transformative experience reconnecting me with my essence and the natural world. Though emotions from the dive still swirled within, I sensed this experience had altered me in significant, yet indeterminate ways. The underwater realm had offered me a glimpse into a divine creation that had felt distant before— a poignant reminder of life's interconnectedness and a lasting peace that I would carry within always.

10

THE PROMISE OF FUTURE DIVES

Returning to shore, I found myself immersed in deep reflection on the significant impact of the dive. What had begun as a recreational activity had transformed into a sacred ritual—a journey of healing and self-discovery in the depths of the ocean. Each dive, including the one just completed, offered me not only an opportunity to explore the wonders of the underwater world but also a chance to reconnect with myself and draw strength from the serene solitude beneath the waves.

As the boat gently rocked with the rhythm of the waves, I felt a sense of tranquility wash over me. The horizon stretched endlessly before us, where the sea met the sky in a seamless blend of blue hues, mirroring the boundless possibilities unfolding in my journey of personal growth and healing.

➤ Finding Healing in the Depths

Descending into the ocean's embrace, I experienced an immense calmness as the weightlessness of the water enveloped my body. Each breath synchronized with the gentle currents, fostering a deeper connection to the underwater world around me. It was more than just a physical descent; it was a plunge into the depths of my being—a journey to confront fears and anxieties that had long lingered beneath the surface.

Memories of past struggles surfaced like bubbles rising to meet the sunlight. I recalled the initial apprehension before entering the water, unsure if I could overcome the lingering trauma of my first diving experience. Yet, guided by Sebastian's steady presence and unwavering encouragement, I took the leap into the unknown.

➤ **Embracing Growth and Transformation**

As the dive unfolded, the ocean revealed itself not only as a vast physical landscape but also as a powerful metaphor for my journey of self-discovery. The ebb and flow of the currents mirrored the ebbs and flows of life—each moment presenting its own challenges and opportunities for growth. Amidst the vibrant colors of coral reefs, I found solace in the beauty that emerged from moments of darkness, serving as proof of life's resilience in all its manifestations.

With each stroke through the water, I felt a renewed sense of purpose and clarity. The challenges I encountered underwater paralleled those in my life—each obstacle an opportunity to learn, grow, and emerge stronger than before. It was a reminder that growth and healing are not linear processes, but continuous journeys of self-reflection and renewal.

➤ **A Promise to Myself**

Looking ahead to future dives, a sense of anticipation and excitement filled me. The underwater world beckoned with its mysteries and wonders, each dive promising a new chapter in my ongoing journey of healing and self-discovery. I made a silent promise to myself—not just to seek the peace and clarity of the ocean's depths, but to carry those transformative lessons into my daily life. This promise was a testament to the powerful impact of the underwater world, inspiring others to embark on their own paths of growth and healing.

> ### The Journey Continues

Returning to the island, I understood this dive marked only the beginning of a profound transformation. With its ever-changing currents and boundless beauty, the ocean revealed that growth and healing were ongoing processes, each dive unveiling new layers of understanding and inner peace.

Stepping off the boat with my husband and daughter by my side, I realized this journey was not one I undertook alone. Their unwavering support and presence had been integral to my healing process, enriching our shared experiences and forging connections that would endure a lifetime.

➤ Commitment to Independence

Yet, true growth demanded a commitment to independence in my diving skills. While Sebastian's guidance remained invaluable, achieving self-reliance in the underwater world would enhance my experiences and empower me in new ways.

Determined to hone my skills, I resolved to become proficient and self-reliant in navigating the ocean's depths. The path ahead was clear: embrace challenges, continue learning and growing, and dive with the confidence that I could explore the depths independently.

This commitment to independence marked the next phase of my transformative journey—an acknowledgement of the strength and resilience I had discovered within myself.

Standing on the shore, gazing at the vast expanse of water, I knew I would return to its depths time and again. Each dive would bring new insights and discoveries, reinforcing the lessons of courage, resilience, and self-discovery that shaped my life, both above and below the surface.

➤ The Promise of Future Dives

The ocean had become my teacher, guiding me through life's turbulent waters and revealing beauty to those willing to dive deep. With each dive, I continued to explore, learn, and grow— embracing the promise of the future with an open heart and a steadfast determination to find peace and solace in the depths.

11

PERSONAL GROWTH AND HEALING

Reflecting on my transformative journey, I am overwhelmed by the profound sense of growth and healing that has washed over me. Memories once steeped in trauma and fear now shimmer with a newfound peace and acceptance.

Returning to the ocean's depths proved to be the catalyst for this metamorphosis—a symphony of conquering fears, rediscovering a lost part of myself, and learning to embrace the healing power of vulnerability.

The underwater world, once a source of anxiety, reemerged as my sanctuary. Its silent beauty and haunting tranquility offered solace as I descended into the azure depths. Each gentle ripple of the water seemed to echo the rhythms of my heart, a poignant reminder of the inextricable link between inner peace and the serenity of the sea. Sebastian, my steadfast guide through these emotional currents, became more than just a diving instructor; he became a mentor, imparting lessons that transcended mere diving skills. He taught me the power of trust—not just in him, but in the incredible strength and resilience that resided within me.

In those quiet moments suspended beneath the waves, I confronted the shadows of my past. Echoes of old anxieties and traumas resurfaced, threatening to pull me back into the darkness. Yet, with each measured breath through my regulator, I felt a renewed sense of purpose and resolve. This journey wasn't just about mastering the art of diving; it was about reclaiming my sense of self-worth and inner peace.

The sunlit coral reefs, teeming with life and color, became a kaleidoscope, reflecting the whirlwind of emotions churning within me. Schools of fish darted around me in a mesmerizing ballet, their synchronized movements serving as a beautiful reminder of the harmony found in the most unexpected corners of the world. I marveled at nature's intricate dance unfolding before my eyes, each creature playing a vital role in the ocean's delicate ecosystem.

But it wasn't just the vibrant marine life that captivated me—it was the silent lessons they imparted about empathy, kindness, and interconnectedness. Just as every fish contributed to the vibrant tapestry of the reef, so did every person contribute their unique thread to the rich fabric of human experience. Sebastian's unwavering dedication to sharing his love for diving resonated deeply, reminding me of the power of genuine connection and shared passions.

Navigating the underwater world with newfound confidence, I encountered challenges that tested my resilience and determination. The unpredictable currents mirrored the turbulent storms I had weathered in life. Yet, with Sebastian's patient guidance and unwavering support as my anchor, I learned to navigate these currents with grace and courage. His unwavering support became a beacon of hope in moments of uncertainty, reminding me of the strength I possessed even when doubt threatened to cloud my judgment.

Above all, this journey was a significant lesson in the power of vulnerability. By confronting my deepest fears and embracing the unknown, I discovered a wellspring of strength within myself that I had long believed lost. The scars of past traumas transformed from badges of shame into badges of honor, a testament to the battles fought and the victories won.

In the quiet depths of the ocean, I found not just solace, but renewal. Each dive became a pilgrimage of self-discovery, revealing the remarkable resilience of the human spirit.

The sea, with its boundless depths and timeless beauty, mirrored the depths of my soul, inviting exploration, healing, and growth. Emerging from the dive, I carried a newfound sense of purpose and clarity. The fears that once held me captive had transformed into sources of strength and unwavering resilience. I had learned not only to survive, but to thrive in the face of adversity, embracing life's challenges as opportunities for growth and transformation.

Looking back on my journey, I realize that healing is not a destination, but a continuous evolution—a journey of self-discovery and self-compassion. The ocean taught me the importance of listening to my inner voice, of honoring my fears while refusing to let them dictate my path. Each dive was a step toward healing, reclaiming the joy and wonder buried beneath layers of doubt and insecurity.

This experience left me with a renewed sense of purpose and a deep appreciation for the interconnectedness of all life. Just as the ocean's ecosystems rely on each other for balance and harmony, so do we rely on each other for support and understanding. This journey taught me the power of empathy, of reaching out a hand to those in need, and embracing the beauty of human connection.

Ultimately, the most significant lesson I learned was the power of trusting in the healing force of love—love for oneself, love for others, and love for the natural world that sustains us all. As I continue this journey of self-discovery, I carry the lessons learned beneath the waves close to my heart—serving as a reminder of personal growth, healing, and the profound interconnectedness of all living beings.

12

THE LASTING IMPACT

The impact of this transformative journey extended far beyond the dive itself, touching every facet of my life. It altered my perspective on existence, deepened my reverence for the natural world, and strengthened my bonds with others. I became more mindful, present, and attuned to the beauty and wonder surrounding me, aspiring for the lessons learned underwater to guide my daily interactions and approach to challenges.

In the tranquil aftermath of the dive, with the sun descending towards the horizon, I reflected on the profound changes this odyssey had wrought within me. The ocean had become both a crucible of challenge and a haven of healing, where transformation had unfolded before my eyes. Its depths mirrored the depths of my soul, revealing truths and insights long buried beneath the surface.

Seated on the shore, attuned to the rhythmic cadence of the waves, I felt an immense gratitude for the journey that had led me here. Each wave seemed to whisper secrets of resilience and renewal, reminding me of the inherent strength within and the boundless possibilities awaiting beyond the horizon. The rhythmic crashing of the waves became a metaphor for life's ebbs and flows, reinforcing the lessons of persistence and hope.

The days following the dive brimmed with renewed purpose and clarity. This journey underscored the importance of resilience, inner fortitude, and the transformative power of empathy and kindness. Inspired to share these revelations, I sought to encourage others on their own paths of growth and healing, fostering a deeper appreciation for our place within the natural world. I felt an urgent need to convey the profound peace and clarity the ocean had given me.

Translating these experiences into words became my mission, aiming to create a narrative that resonated universally. Through my writing, I endeavored to reach those grappling with fears and uncertainties, offering them a glimpse of nature's ability to heal and transform. My prose sought to convey the serenity and enlightenment I had discovered beneath the waves, inspiring others to seek their own sanctuaries, whether in nature or within themselves.

My book emerged as a vivid testament to my personal journey, encapsulating the lessons learned and the wisdom gleaned. It celebrated resilience, courage, and nature's enduring capacity to heal and renew. With each chapter penned, I felt a deep sense of fulfillment, hopeful that my experiences might resonate and inspire others on their own paths. I envisioned this narrative as a beacon of hope, illustrating the transformative power of nature and the human spirit's resilience.

Ultimately, this odyssey transcended mere exploration of the ocean's depths; it delved into the depths of my soul. It represented a quest for strength through vulnerability, a celebration of adaptation, and a discovery of life's boundless beauty. Through my storytelling, I aimed to impart these lessons, sparking a ripple effect of healing, growth, and reverence for our shared world. Writing became the conduit between my experiences and the broader human experience, forging connections and contributing to a collective journey toward understanding and harmony.

As I sat down to transcribe my journey, memories surged like currents, carrying with them the emotions, insights, and revelations of my odyssey. Each page bore witness to my heart poured out, an attempt to capture the essence of my experiences and the wisdom gained. This process of introspection and expression was in itself healing, an extension of the voyage that began in the ocean's depths.

In sharing my narrative, I embraced the interconnectedness of humanity, believing that our individual stories resonate and inspire others.

This book stood as my contribution, a portrayal of nature's transformative influence and the resilience of the human spirit. It celebrated life's complexities and beauty, and it underscored the limitless potential for growth and renewal. The act of writing became an extension of my journey, a way to continue the exploration and to invite others to embark on their own paths of discovery and healing.

With the completion of the final chapter, I savored a profound sense of closure and new beginnings. This journey had come full circle— from the depths of the ocean to the depths of my soul and, I hoped, into the hearts and minds of others. The enduring impact of this experience lay not only in the lessons learned but sharing those lessons, forging connections, and inspiring hope and renewal throughout the world.

Reflecting on the transformative power of my journey, I recognized the significance of facing and overcoming one's fears. The dive had been a catalyst for profound personal growth, illustrating that true strength emerges from confronting our deepest vulnerabilities. The ocean, with its vastness and mystery, had served as both a mirror and a mentor, teaching me that the unknown holds not only challenges but also infinite possibilities for growth and enlightenment.

As I continued to share my story, I found it resonated with many who were also seeking meaning and healing in their lives. Individuals reached out, sharing their own experiences of transformation and expressing gratitude for the inspiration my journey provided. This feedback reinforced my belief in the power of storytelling as a tool for connection and healing. It underscored the idea that while our journeys are unique, the themes of resilience, courage, and renewal are universal.

The process of writing and sharing my narrative also deepened my appreciation for the natural world. I became more attuned to the subtle rhythms of nature, finding solace and inspiration in its beauty and resilience. This heightened awareness translated into a more mindful and intentional way of living, as I sought to honor and protect the environment that had given me so much.

In the end, this book was more than just a recounting of a dive; it was a celebration of life's journey and the profound lessons it offers. It was a reminder that within each of us lies a reservoir of strength and wisdom, waiting to be uncovered through our experiences. By embracing vulnerability and seeking connection, we can navigate the depths of our own souls and emerge with a deeper understanding of ourselves and the world around us.

The lasting impact of this journey was not confined to the pages of a book; it permeated every aspect of my life. It influenced how I approached challenges, interacted with others, and viewed the world. The dive had been a transformative experience, but its true power lay in the ripple effects it created, inspiring others to embark on their own journeys of discovery and healing.

As I concluded my writing, I felt a deep sense of fulfillment and purpose. This journey has revealed the enduring power of nature and the human spirit, a celebration of life's beauty and resilience. Through my story, I hoped to continue inspiring others, fostering a deeper appreciation for our interconnectedness and the boundless potential for growth and renewal that lies within each of us.

EPILOGUE

A JOURNEY OF TRANSFORMATION

Standing on the shore, I gazed out at the vast expanse of the ocean, its waves gently lapping against the sand. The journey back into the depths had been more than a mere return to diving; it had been a voyage of self-discovery, healing, and transformation.

The memories of those initial dives with Rick, filled with fear and inadequacy, had once haunted me. But through my husband's unwavering support and Sebastian's compassionate guidance, I found the strength to confront and overcome those fears. Once a source of anxiety, the ocean had become a sanctuary of peace and reflection.

Sebastian's passion for the underwater world, empathy, and ability to connect deeply have shown me the power of trust and the beauty of embracing vulnerability. The dive with him was not just a physical descent, but a journey into my depths, unearthing emotions and memories that had long been buried.

As I swam alongside vibrant coral and curious sea creatures, I felt a profound connection to the ocean and my life's journey. The ocean's rhythmic ebb and flow mirrored the cycles of my own experiences, reminding me that even the darkest depths could be illuminated with patience and courage.

I found a renewed sense of purpose and clarity in the tranquil embrace of the sea. The lessons learned beneath the waves transcended the underwater realm, permeating every aspect of my life. I realized that overcoming fear and finding peace was not a destination but an ongoing process—a continuous journey of growth, resilience, and self-compassion.

Returning to the surface after each dive, I emerged as a diver and a person transformed. The ocean had given me the gift of perspective, teaching me to navigate life's challenges with grace and to cherish the moments of joy and connection.

Reflecting on this journey, I am grateful for my husband, Sebastian, and the ocean itself. The depths that once symbolized fear now represent hope, healing, and endless possibilities.

My story, *Revisiting the Depths: Overcoming Fear and Finding Peace - A Journey of Transformation*, is a testament to the power of facing our fears, trusting in the support of others, and embracing the journey of self-discovery. It invites all who read it to dive into their depths, confront their fears, and find the peace that lies within.

The ocean continues to call to me—a reminder that beneath the surface of our fears lies a world of wonder and potential. As I look toward the horizon, I am ready to embrace whatever comes next, knowing I can navigate any depths and find my way to the surface.

The moments spent beneath the waves linger in my mind, each dive leaving an indelible mark on my soul. I carry with me the echoes of marine life dancing around me; the sunlight filtering through the water, casting ethereal patterns on the seabed. These memories are not just snapshots of beauty but remarkable lessons in resilience and interconnectedness.

As I navigate daily life, I find myself returning to the lessons learned in the depths. The ocean taught me patience as I waited for the perfect moment to capture a glimpse of a shy sea creature. It taught me humility as I witnessed the grandeur of the underwater landscapes, far beyond my ability to fully comprehend or control. Most importantly, it taught me gratitude for the simple joys—a clear day on the boat, the laughter of fellow divers, and the warmth of a supportive hand in moments of uncertainty.

Looking ahead, I carry a compelling sense of purpose born from this transformative journey. I am inspired to share my story, not just as a narrative of personal triumph, but as a beacon of hope for those grappling with their own fears and uncertainties. The ocean's enduring embrace continues to guide me, reminding me of the boundless strength that lies within and the infinite possibilities that await those willing to dive deep.

ACKNOWLEDGEMENTS

Writing this book has been an incredible journey, and I thank God for providing me with the strength, inspiration, and perseverance to complete it.

I am deeply grateful to those who have supported me along the way:

To my husband, Eugene, your support and love have been invaluable. Thank you for encouraging and believing in me.

To my children, Emily and Daniel, your love and patience have been my greatest source of strength.

To the talented team behind this book and audiobook—editor, formatter, book cover designer, marketing consultant, audiobook narrator, and producer—your collective dedication and expertise have been invaluable. Thank you for your hard work and commitment to bringing this project to life.

To my readers, thank you for embarking on this journey with me. Your support means the world to me.

ABOUT THE AUTHOR

Amy Tan is an accomplished business executive and award winning author with over twenty years of experience in corporate leadership and market expansion across Southeast Asia. She holds a Business Administration degree from the Royal Melbourne Institute of Technology and a Postgraduate Certificate from the University of Nottingham.

Beyond her corporate role, Amy is a passionate storyteller, weaving her diverse experiences into narratives that explore personal growth, resilience, and transformation. Her latest book, *Revisiting the Depths - Overcoming Fear and Finding Peace,* which won the Literary Titan Gold Book Award, recounts her emotional and spiritual journey as she overcomes a long-held fear of the ocean through diving.

Her other works, including *Doing Business in ASEAN* and *China: An Ultimate Guide to Doing*

Business, showcase her expertise in regional economic integration. Having lived in Malaysia, Thailand, the Philippines, and Indonesia, Amy brings a rich, cross-cultural perspective to her writing, inspiring readers to overcome challenges and make positive changes. Her work highlights the powerful impact of storytelling on personal and professional development.

COMING SOON!

From My Heart to Yours - Life Lessons for My Son

A Purpose-Value Driven Life and Lasting Legacy

www.amytanbooks.com